Five Nights at Freddy's™
SURVIVAL ~~SECURITY~~ LOGBOOK

Based on the series Five Nights at Freddy's, created by Scott Cawthon

Photos © Shutterstock: cover blood spots and throughout (Gl0ck);
cover brown texture (homydesign); cover beige texture (NataLT); 1 background and throughout (alexandre17);
2 center (Lyudmyla Kharlamova); 3 coffee ring and throughout (Africa Studio); 42 center (Alexandr III);
42 bottom left and right (olllikeballoon); 43 top (Ksenya Savva); 43 right (olllikeballoon); 43 bottom (Studio_G);
52 bottom (Lyudmyla Kharlamova); 64 tape and throughout (jocic).

ISBN 978-1-338-22930-1

20 19 18 17 16 15 14   23 24 25 26 27

Printed in China   62

First printing 2018
Art by Tina Francisco and Katrina Mae Hao
Book design by Carolyn Bull

THIS BOOK BELONGS TO:

~~MIKE~~

Sorry—looks like somebody's
already written in this one . . .
You don't mind, right?

HOW TO USE THIS
LOGBOOK

Welcome to the first day of your exciting new career! This journal was designed for you, Fazbear Entertainment's newest employee, to both welcome you and ensure you feel fulfilled and prepared during your first week on the job. We don't want you to feel overwhelmed, otherwise you might not come back!

After each night's work, we ask that you take a moment for self-reflection by completing the various activities in the pages that follow. Some of these activities will review your training, while others will help you clear your mind and focus. And, of course, don't forget to log any strange events that occur throughout your shift.

Let's get started!

NIGHT 1:
A THRILLING NEW CHAPTER!

To begin, we suggest you fill out some basic information in the unlikely event of an emergency. All set? Please cut out this contact card and return it to your supervisor at the end of your first shift.

Name:

Phone:

Address:

Medications:

Allergies:

Organ Donor:

End-of-Life Preferences:

In case of emergency, please contact:

Name:

Phone:

Relation:

Feeling down? Don't!

List ten reasons why applying to Freddy Fazbear's Pizza seemed like a good idea at the time.

1. _Employees get free pizza._

2. _____

3. _____

4. _____

5. _____

6. _____

7. _____

8. _____

9. _____

   _____

10. _____

   _____

Would You Rather . . .

 Hug Freddy? . . . or . . . Hug Foxy?

Work day shift with
two parties? . . . or . . . Work night shift
and clean up?

 Play guitar with Bonnie? . . . or . . . Sing with Freddy?

Listen to Ballora's
music all night? . . . or . . . Listen to the Puppet's
music box all night?

 Get an ice cream
from Circus Baby? . . . or . . . Get a cupcake
from Chica?

If you were going to design a new animatronic friend for the kids at one of Fazbear Entertainment's numerous enterprises, what would it look like? What special features might it have?

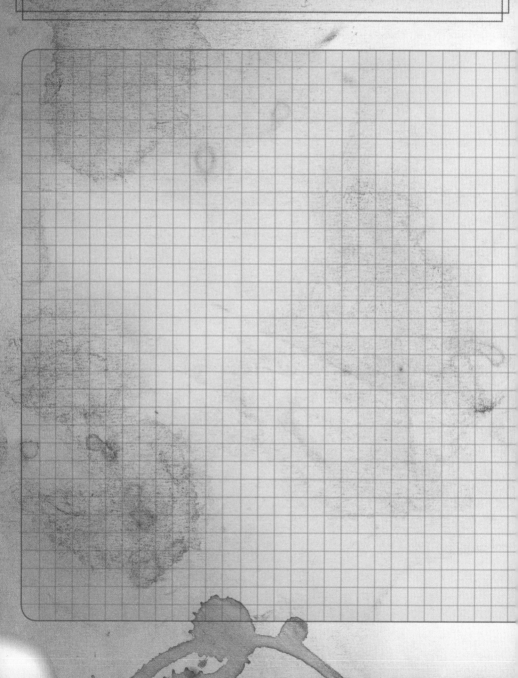

Special Features:

_____

_____

_____

_____

_____

Quiz: Reviewing Your Training

Have you listened carefully to all the night guard training tapes? Test your knowledge here and see how you fared on page 12.

1. What's our motto at Freddy Fazbear's Pizza?

   a. A mystical place for kids and parents, where fantasy and intrigue come to light

   b. A magical place for kids and grown-ups alike, where fantasy and fun come to life

   c. A magnificent place for kids and grown-ups alike, where fun comes to life

2. Fazbear Entertainment is not responsible for damage to . . .

   a. Property or person

   b. Animatronics

   c. Kitchen equipment

3. Why are the animatronics left in free-roaming mode at night?

   a. There is no way to turn them off.

   b. They need to blow off some steam at the end of the day.

   c. Their servos lock up if they are turned off for too long.

4. If the animatronics see you after hours, they'll most likely believe you're . . .

    a. A metal endoskeleton without its costume on

    b. A security guard

    c. A child in need of a hug

5. Why should you only close the doors and operate the lights/cameras when absolutely necessary?

    a. We are currently involved in an "eco-friendly" initiative.

    b. The building has limited power supply between 12 and 6 a.m.

    c. The animatronics are drawn to the light.

6. Where are the most crucial blind spots in your cameras?

    a. The kitchen

    b. Outside Pirate Cove

    c. Right outside the office doors

Quiz Results: How Did You Do?

Tally up your score!

1. Correct answer: b.   4. Correct answer: a.

2. Correct answer: a.   5. Correct answer: b.

3. Correct answer: c.   6. Correct answer: c.

2 or fewer correct answers

Are you sure this is the job for you? You made some serious errors in your responses. Please thoroughly review your training before returning tomorrow.

3–4 correct answers

Your answers were partially correct, but we recommend brushing up on some of your responsibilities before your next shift. After all, one mistake could have dire consequences.

5 or more correct answers SURVIVAL

You have the best chances for ~~success~~ in this position. Job well done!

When you're scared, it can sometimes help to imagine what you fear in a funny way. Let's try it out—sketch and color in a silly costume for the Puppet to wear.

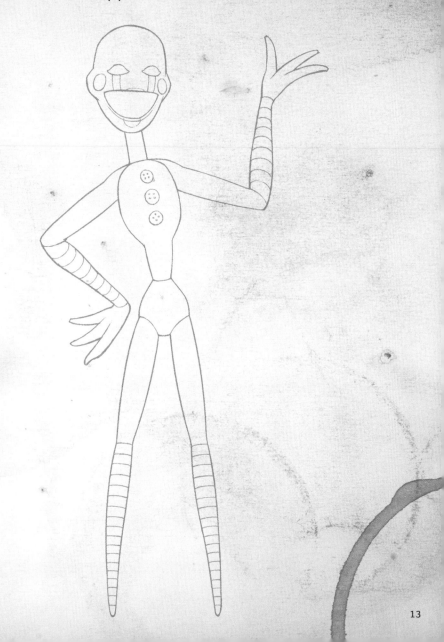

You know what they say—laugh and the world laughs with you. Cry and you cry alone. Make up some jokes for Freddy and his friends to make you laugh on the next page!

not FUNNY!!

15

Working the night shift can be hard, especially when the people closest to you work daylight hours. List the five people you most want to see at the end of the day.

1. _____

2. _____

3. _____

4. _____

5. _____

Who would you recommend for this job?

_____

_____

_____

_____

_____

_____

_____

_____

Take your family OUT . . .
for a night of fun at
Freddy Fazbear's Pizza!

Perfect Pizza Pack

Offer not valid when combined with other offers.

- TWO medium pizzas with your choice of TWO toppings each
- 15 game/ride tokens
- 1 pitcher of soda

FREDDY FAZBEAR'S PIZZA

Freddy's Fun Time

Offer not valid when combined with other offers.

- 30 game/ride tokens
- One large pizza with an additional topping
- 1 pitcher of soda

FREDDY FAZBEAR'S PIZZA

Foxy's Pirate-Palooza

Offer not valid when combined with other offers.

- Visit from Foxy at Pirate Cove
- 45 game/ride tokens
- 12 novelty eye patches

FREDDY FAZBEAR'S PIZZA

Make your workspace feel like home! What decorations can you add to your desk to make the space feel more cozy?

As a child, what did you want to be when you grew up?
How does this differ from your current job prospects?

_____

_____

_____

_____

_____

_____

_____

WHAT DO YOU REMEMBER?

_____

_____

_____

_____

_____

_____

_____

_____

_____

_____

Balloons!

Imagine that you've received a promising new opportunity to become a manager at a Freddy Fazbear's Pizza. It's up to you to make the big decisions that keep our customers coming back. Try making some of these decisions in the space below.

1. Would you make more human or animal animatronics?

   _____

2. Would your animatronic friends be shiny and glossy, or soft and fuzzy?

   _____

3. Which would you serve the most of—cupcakes, ice cream, or pizza?

   _____

4. Would you give Circus Baby a hug if she gave you an ice cream cone?

   _____

Make a bucket list of all the things you'd most like to do in life. What is holding you back from doing them? You never know how much time you have left!

1. _____

2. _____

3. _____

4. _____

5. _____

6. _____

7. _____

8. _____

9. _____

10. _____

After your first night on the job, we bet you're feeling pretty grateful to be alive. Reflect on the things in life that you are most thankful for.

_____

_____

_____

_____

_____

_____

WAS YOUR FAVORITE
CHILDHOOD TOY A PLASTIC
PURPLE TELEPHONE?

_____

_____

_____

_____

_____

_____

EVENT LOG: NIGHT 1

Please report any unusual events in the space below.

INCIDENT REPORT

Date: _____ Time: _____ a.m./p.m.

Night Guard on Duty: _____

Person(s) Involved: _____

Animatronic(s) Involved: _____

Description of Events: _____

_____

Injury ☐ Property Damage ☐ Death ☐

Missing Persons ☐ Police Involved ☐

Signature _____

INCIDENT REPORT

Date: _____ Time: _____ a.m./p.m.

Night Guard on Duty: _____

Person(s) Involved: _____

Animatronic(s) Involved: _____

Description of Events: _____

_____

Injury ☐ Property Damage ☐ Death ☐

Missing Persons ☐ Police Involved ☐

Signature _____

INCIDENT REPORT

Date: _____ Time: _____ a.m./p.m.

Night Guard on Duty: _____

Person(s) Involved: _____

Animatronic(s) Involved: _____

Description of Events: _____

_____

Injury ☐ Property Damage ☐ Death ☐

Missing Persons ☐ Police Involved ☐

Signature _____

Feelings About Tonight's Shift

Please circle how you would rate your feelings on a scale of 1–10, with 10 being the best, and 1 being the worst, on the scale below.

Overall: 1 2 3 4 5 6 7 8 9 10

Fulfillment: 1 2 3 4 5 6 7 8 9 10

Health: 1 2 3 4 5 6 7 8 9 10

Stress: 1 2 3 4 5 6 7 8 9 10

Purpose: 1 2 3 4 5 6 7 8 9 10

Hope: 1 2 3 4 5 6 7 8 9 10

Existential   1 2 3 4 5 6 7 8 9 10
Dread:

NIGHT 2:
ANOTHER CHANCE TO SHINE!

Employment is vital to any well-functioning society.
List ten reasons why you really need this job.

1. _____

2. _____

3. _____

4. _____

5. _____

6. _____

7. _____

8. _____

9. _____

10. _____

If you were a child, what prizes would you want to see behind the prize counter? Draw them here.

It's important to have heroes to aspire to. List your favorite characters from movies, books, and television who showed bravery in the face of extreme obstacles. Can you relate your current experiences to their heroic journeys?

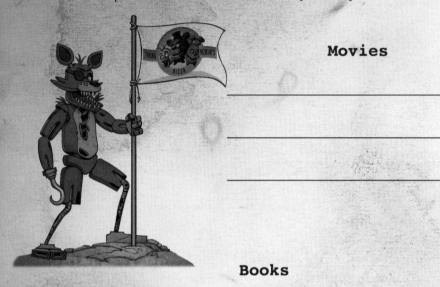

Movies

_____

_____

_____

Books

_____

_____

_____

Television

Clara from "The Immortal and the Restless" because everything about this place is crazy

and no one seems to notice except me.

_____

Reflect on the happiest day of your life. Write about one specific memory from that day that will make you feel better if you find yourself facing ~~new difficulties.~~
CERTAIN DEATH!!

_____
_____
_____
_____
_____
_____
_____
_____
_____
_____
_____

DO YOU REMEMBER YOUR NAME?

One way to find hope in a seemingly hopeless situation
is to fast-forward and try peeking into the future.
Let's give it a try—what will your life look like in five years?

Take a BITE . . .
out of fun
On your next birthday!

Chica's Cupcake Chaos

Offer not valid when combined with other offers.

- 12 cupcakes
- 20 game/ride tokens
- Custom Party Kit with invitations and hats

Birthday Ball

Offer not valid when combined with other offers.

- 24 balloons
- 20 game/ride tokens
- Custom Party Kit with invitations and hats

Happiest Day

Offer not valid when combined with other offers.

- Reserved Party Room
- Three-tier birthday cake
- Receive a gift from the Puppet
- Custom Party Kit with invitations and hats

To help you reach a more stable and relaxing frame of mind, write down your favorite **therapeutic musical** selections. Please note that some animatronics are audio-activated, so refrain from playing music in the workplace.

_____ / _____
　　　　　　(song)　　　　　　　　　　　　　　　(artist)

_____ / _____
　　　　　　(song)　　　　　　　　　　　　　　　(artist)

_____ / _____
　　　　　　(song)　　　　　　　　　　　　　　　(artist)

_____ / _____
　　　　　　(song)　　　　　　　　　　　　　　　(artist)

casual bongos

If you had to survive in a small crawl space under a desk for a week while surrounded by baby-themed animatronics, **would you rather . . .**

Sleep with one eye open? . . . or . . . Not sleep at all?

Eat only baked beans? . . . or . . . Eat only tuna salad?

Make a plan to escape? . . . or . . . Make a plan to call for help?

Listen to a creepy voice? . . . or . . . Listen to the silence?

Lose your frontal lobe? . . . or . . . Lose an arm?

Make an exercise schedule! Working out can keep your mind healthy, too, speeding up reaction times that are key to success in your new position. Plan some activities for the week.

MONDAY

8 a.m. _____   1 p.m. _____
9 a.m. _____   2 p.m. _____
10 a.m. _____   3 p.m. _____
11 a.m. _____   4 p.m. _____
12 p.m. _____   5 p.m. _____

TUESDAY

8 a.m. _____   1 p.m. _____
9 a.m. _____   2 p.m. _____
10 a.m. _____   3 p.m. _____
11 a.m. _____   4 p.m. _____
12 p.m. _____   5 p.m. _____

WEDNESDAY

8 a.m. _____   1 p.m. _____
9 a.m. _____   2 p.m. _____
10 a.m. _____   3 p.m. _____
11 a.m. _____   4 p.m. _____
12 p.m. _____   5 p.m. _____

THURSDAY

8 a.m. _____	1 p.m. _____
9 a.m. _____	2 p.m. _____
10 a.m. _____	3 p.m. _____
11 a.m. _____	4 p.m. _____
12 p.m. _____	5 p.m. _____

FRIDAY

8 a.m. _____	1 p.m. _____
9 a.m. _____	2 p.m. _____
10 a.m. _____	3 p.m. _____
11 a.m. _____	4 p.m. _____
12 p.m. _____	5 p.m. _____

SATURDAY

8 a.m. _____	1 p.m. _____		
9 a.m. _____	2 p.m. _____		
10 a.m. _____	3 p.m. _____		
11 a.m. _____	4 p.m. _____		
12 p.m. _____	5 p.m. _____		

SUNDAY

8 a.m. _____	1 p.m. _____		
9 a.m. _____	2 p.m. _____		
10 a.m. _____	3 p.m. _____		
11 a.m. _____	4 p._____		
12 p.m. _____	5 p.m. _____		

Workout Suggestions

- Run five miles
- Run even faster
- Take a self-defense class

Think about some steps you can take to improve your productivity at work.

Step 1:

Step 2:

Step 3:

Helpful hint: Cutting down on distractions is key to noticing subtle changes in your environment. These subtle changes
are often the forerunner of ~~security~~ threats.
animatronic

Draw yourself as an animatronic. What special abilities would you have?

_____

_____

_____

_____

_____

_____

_____

Studies show that you forget half of your dreams in the first five minutes after waking. Use this page and the next page to sketch and write notes about your **recent dreams**. Reflect on the meaning of your dreams.

DO YOU HAVE DREAMS?

DO ANY OF THESE TOYS LOOK
FAMILIAR TO YOU?

MY NAME

ONE OF THESE
BELONG TO YOU?

43

Story Starter: Where's Foxy?

Flex your creative muscles by writing your own short story in the space below. You can use this starting prompt to kick your imagination into high gear.

* *

I checked the security cameras, cycling through the feeds until I came back to Pirate Cove once again. Where could Foxy be? Suddenly I heard a *thud, thud, thud,* like the heavy pounding of animatronic footsteps. I turned to my left, and . . .

_____

_____

_____

_____

_____

_____

_____

_____

_____

_____

_____

_____

_____

EVENT LOG: NIGHT 2

Please report any unusual events in the space below.

INCIDENT REPORT

Date: _____ Time: _____ a.m./p.m.

Night Guard on Duty: _____

Person(s) Involved: _____

Animatronic(s) Involved: _____

Description of Events: _____

_____

Injury ☐ Property Damage ☐ Death ☐

Missing Persons ☐ Police Involved ☐

Signature _____

INCIDENT REPORT

Date: _____ Time: _____ a.m./p.m.

Night Guard on Duty: _____

Person(s) Involved: _____

Animatronic(s) Involved: _____

Description of Events: _____

_____

Injury ☐ Property Damage ☐ Death ☐

Missing Persons ☐ Police Involved ☐

Signature _____

INCIDENT REPORT

Date: _____ Time: _____ a.m./p.m.

Night Guard on Duty: _____

Person(s) Involved: _____

Animatronic(s) Involved: _____

Description of Events: _____

_____

Injury ☐ Property Damage ☐ Death ☐

Missing Persons ☐ Police Involved ☐

Signature _____

Feelings About Tonight's Shift

Please circle how you would rate your feelings on a scale of 1–10, with 10 being the best, and 1 being the worst, on the scale below.

Overall: 1 2 3 4 5 6 7 8 9 10

Fulfillment: 1 2 3 4 5 6 7 8 9 10

Health: 1 2 3 4 5 6 7 8 9 10

Stress: 1 2 3 4 5 6 7 8 9 10

Purpose: 1 2 3 4 5 6 7 8 9 10

Hope: 1 2 3 7 2 6 7 8 9 10

Existential
Dread: 1 2 3 4 5 6 7 8 9 10

Welcome back to another pivotal night of your thriving new career, where you get to really ask yourself, "What am I doing with my life? What would my friends say?" And most importantly, "Will I ever see my family again?" **Let's get started by listing ten bad habits you'd like to break.**

1. <u>Chewing gum excessively.</u>

2. _____

3. _____

4. _____

5. _____

6. _____

7. _____

8. _____

9. _____

10. _____

Quiz: Operating Spring Lock Suits

Did you review the training tapes about our new spring lock suits? Remember: You must review this vital training before interacting with a spring lock suit/animatronic.

1. What makes a spring lock suit different from a standard animatronic?

    a. It can make ice cream and inflate balloons.

    b. It's more dangerous than the standard animatronic.

    c. It doubles as both an animatronic and a mascot costume.

2. While in animatronic mode, spring lock suits walk toward what?

    a. Light

    b. Sound

    c. Birthday cake

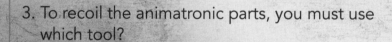

3. To recoil the animatronic parts, you must use which tool?

    a. A handcrank

    b. Your fingers

    c. A wrench

4. Which of the following should you not do to the spring locks?

    a. Breathe on them

    b. Touch them

    c. All of the above

5. If you trip the spring locks, what should you do?

    a. Die in front of customers

    b. Scream for help

    c. Head to an offstage area before bleeding out

6. Failing to follow the rules may result in what?

    a. Firing

    b. Accidents/injury/death/irreparable and grotesque maiming

    c. Promotion

Quiz Results: How Did You Do?

Tally up your score!

1. Correct answer: c.   4. Correct answer: c.

2. Correct answer: b.   5. Correct answer: c.

3. Correct answer: a.   6. Correct answer: b.

2 or fewer correct answers
Please review your training before you even look at another spring lock suit, and *don't* speak to any insurance agents should you encounter them.

3–4 correct answers
You gave some half-right answers here. We recommend reviewing your training with the audiocassette tapes.

5 or more correct answers
You paid attention! You may not need to wear a spring lock suit as part of your night guard duties, but you know how to handle a spring lock animatronic if you encounter it.

*Disregard this quiz—
in fact, don't mention the
spring lock suits to anyone.*

Even the animatronics get stressed out sometimes. Imagine you were going to send the animatronics on vacation. Where would you send each one?

Freddy: _____

Why: _____

_____

Chica: _____

Why: _____

_____

Bonnie: _____

Why: _____

_____

Foxy: _____

Why: _____

_____

During your first week on the job, it can be hard to keep the rules straight, so we've made you this handy checklist!

+ DO follow custom rules for specified animatronics
+ DO listen carefully for new/unfamiliar sounds
+ DO monitor systems and animatronics as necessary
+ DO avoid the animatronics to the best of your ability

- DON'T stare at the camera feeds for too long
- DON'T admit any prior employees

Design a new and advanced endoskeleton.

List some things that would be great to have in a pizzeria that would distract people from the depressing realities of life.

_____
_____
_____
_____
WAS YOUR FAVORITE RIDE THE CAROUSEL?
_____
_____
_____
_____
_____
_____
_____
_____
_____
_____
_____
_____
_____
_____
_____

Create a new game for kids to play with Ballora.
Remember, Ballora inspires kids to get fit and enjoy pizza!

How to Play:

_____
_____
_____
_____
_____
_____
_____
_____
_____
_____
_____
_____
_____
_____
_____
_____

Word Search

See if you can spot all the Fazbear Entertainment–related words in the jumble below!

```
I T S M S E I T S M E I G T W
S M E I C T S M E I T S U M H
E I C T I S M E I T S M A E O
I T A S T M P L A Y E I R T A
S M K E O I T F O X Y S D M R
E I E T B S M E I T B S M E E
L I T S O M E I T S O M E I Y
E T S M R E I T S M N E I T O
T S A M N E I T S M N E I T U
S S Z M O E F I C H I C A T S
E M Z E T I U Y D D E R F T S
A M I E F I N T S M E I T S M
T E P I A T S M E I P A R T Y
T S M E L A U G H I T S M E I
W H A T I S Y O U R N A M E T
```

Afton Robotics   Chica   Party   Foxy

Freddy   Bonnie   Let's Eat   Pizza   Laugh

Fun   Cake   Guard   Play

WHAT DO YOU SEE?

If the animatronics could talk, what do you think they would say?
Use the comic panels below to illustrate your own comic about Freddy and Foxy.

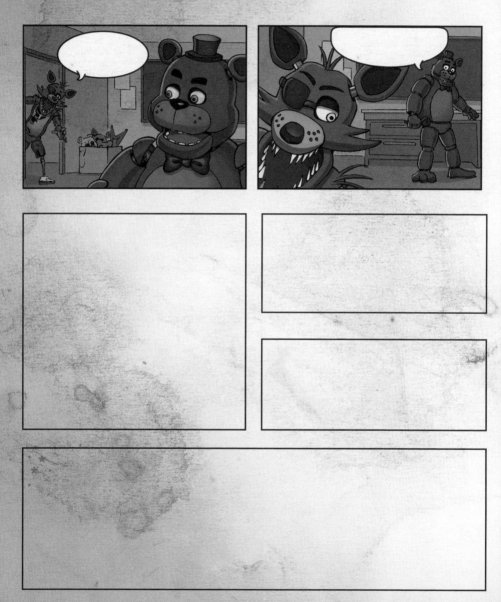

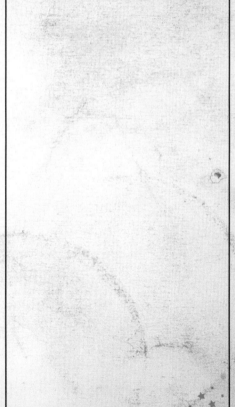

Fazbear Entertainment is often looking to rebrand
whenever a PR disaster strikes.
Use the space below to design a new logo!

SLICE . . .

up some family fun at

Freddy Fazbear's Pizza!

Bonnie's Blast

Hungry Fazbear

Party Time!

You're part of the Fazbear family now! Draw yourself into the photos below.

EVENT LOG: NIGHT 3

Please report any unusual events in the space below.

INCIDENT REPORT

Date: _____ Time: _____ a.m./p.m.

Night Guard on Duty: _____

Person(s) Involved: _____

Animatronic(s) Involved: _____

Description of Events: _____

_____

Injury ☐ Property Damage ☐ Death ☐

Missing Persons ☐ Police Involved ☐

Signature _____

INCIDENT REPORT

Date: _____ Time: _____ a.m./p.m.

Night Guard on Duty: _____

Person(s) Involved: _____

Animatronic(s) Involved: _____

Description of Events: _____

_____

Injury ☐ Property Damage ☐ Death ☐

Missing Persons ☐ Police Involved ☐

Signature _____

INCIDENT REPORT

Date: _____ Time: _____ a.m./p.m.

Night Guard on Duty: _____

Person(s) Involved: _____

Animatronic(s) Involved: _____

Description of Events: _____

_____

Injury ☐ Property Damage ☐ Death ☐

Missing Persons ☐ Police Involved ☐

Signature _____

Feelings About Tonight's Shift

Please circle how you would rate your feelings on a scale of 1–10, with 10 being the best, and 1 being the worst, on the scale below.

Overall: 1 2 3 4 5 6 7 8 9 10

Fulfillment: 1 2 3 4 5 6 7 8 9 10

Health: 1 2 3 4 5 6 7 8 9 10

Stress: 1 2 3 4 5 6 7 8 9 10

Purpose: 1 2 3 4 5 6 7 8 9 10

Hope: 1 2 3 4 5 6 7 8 9 10

Existential   1 2 3 4 5 6 7 8 9 10
Dread:

NIGHT 4:
WHAT ARE YOU
STILL DOING HERE?

What are some poor decisions made by previous
security guards that you will not repeat?

1. _____

2. _____

3. _____

4. _____

5. _____

6. _____

7. _____

8. _____

9. _____

10. _____

If you were to die in a grisly work accident—for instance, being stuffed inside an animatronic suit—who are the people you would miss the most?

"DO YOU MISS THEM?

Write a personal message to each person describing how you met your terrible end, including the animatronic that got you.

Dear _____

_____

_____

_____

_____

_____

Dear _____

_____

_____

_____

_____

_____

Dear _____

_____

_____

_____

_____

_____

Think up an arcade game based on the adventures of the animatronics! Will Foxy sail the seven seas, or will Chica bake a cupcake fit for a king? Write about it here, and then draw a prototype arcade machine.

Game Title: _____

Description: _____
_____
_____
_____

Draw two screenshots from your game!

"POWER"

Uh-oh. This security guard is looking pretty defenseless out in the open after hours. Best draw an animatronic costume on him before he gets stuffed into one!

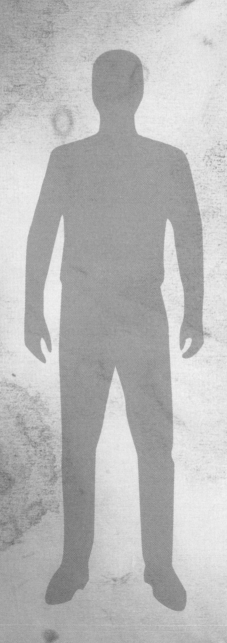

In the face of extreme fear, it can be calming to think back to your childhood. Did you have a stuffed animal or blanket that you took with you everywhere? What about an imaginary friend? Write about them here.

_____

_____

_____

DOES HE STILL TALK
TO YOU?

_____

_____

_____

_____

_____

_____

_____

Quiz: Unlocking Your Potential

Now that you've gotten your bearings, it's time to really test your knowledge. Let's see if you've mastered the job!

1. Over time, you've learned that it's perhaps most important to . . .

    a. Scream when an animatronic approaches.

    b. Make loud noises.

    c. Watch the video feeds.

2. When you hear clanking in the kitchen, it's probably . . .

    a. Foxy

    b. Bonnie

    c. Chica

3. Freddy and his friends tend to become more active . . .

    a. If you check the cameras more often

    b. As the week progresses

    c. If you close the doors

4. Foxy and Bonnie tend to stick to the left side of the restaurant, while Chica and Freddy typically approach from . . .

    a. The right side of the restaurant

    b. Behind you

    c. The left side of the restaurant

5. In general, if you hallucinate seeing strange animatronics while on the job, it's best to . . .

    a. Take a good look at them.

    b. Abandon all hope.

    c. Bring up your video feeds.

6. If you do encounter an animatronic, it's best to refrain from . . .

    a. Making eye contact

    b. Doing a dance

    c. Running away screaming

Quiz Results: How Did You Do?

Tally up your score!

1. Correct answer: c.   4. Correct answer: a.

2. Correct answer: c.   5. Correct answer: c.

3. Correct answer: b.   6. Correct answer: a.

2 or fewer correct answers
Uh-oh. Looks like you've got quite a way to go before you've mastered your duties. You might just need more on-the-job experience, but we're afraid the learning curve is quite steep. Still, we hope you make it long enough to improve!

3–4 correct answers
You're getting there! You may have made a few mistakes in your answers, but it looks like you're starting to catch on.

5 or more correct answers
Wow! While we admit that a person in this unskilled position is usually considered expendable, we're very impressed with how quickly you've mastered your night guard responsibilities.
Well done!

GRAND REOPENING!
Join us at the new
Freddy Fazbear's Pizza!

Bonnie's New Groove

- Special dance party with the animatronics
- Two large pizzas with an additional topping

Freddy's Fancy

- 12 bow ties
- TWO large pizzas with TWO additional toppings
- Two pitchers of soda

Pizza Party Pack

- Three large pizzas, each with an additional topping
- Three pitchers of soda
- 24 cupcakes

For real value, see page 61

Switching to the Day Shift

Flex your creative muscles by writing your own short story in the space below. You can use this starting prompt to kick your imagination into high gear.

I'd only been on night shift for about a week, but I was so relieved to be switched over to the day shift. There's a lot of stress working 12 a.m.—6 a.m. My boss had told me that the animatronics were acting strangely—almost aggressive toward the staff—but I wasn't about to let that scare me off. After work I had an unsettling feeling that I was being followed home . . .

_____
_____
_____
_____
_____
_____
_____
_____
_____
_____
_____

Keep the creativity going by writing a new song for
Freddy and his friends to perform.

_____

_____

_____

_____

_____

_____

_____

_____

_____

_____

Now that you have the song down, draw the animatronics moving to the beat!

IS THIS SONG
FAMILIAR TO YOU?

START

Show Stage

Parts/
Service

Kitchen

FINISH

Freddy Fazbear's Pizza is committed to family fun, and above all—**safety!** By now we're sure you have our Rules for Safety memorized, but are there any that you would add to the list?

RULES FOR SAFETY

1. Don't run.
2. Don't yell.
3. Don't scream.
4. Don't poop on floor.
5. Stay close to mom.
6. Don't touch Freddy.
7. Don't hit.
8. Leave before dark.
9. _____
10. _____
11. _____
12. _____
13. _____
14. _____
15. _____

thank you, management.

Who Would Win?

If the animatronics were battling for control of the pizzeria, who do you think would win and why?

 VS.

Winner: _____

_____

_____

 VS.

Winner: _____

_____

_____

 VS.

Winner: _____

_____

_____

 VS.

Winner: _____

_____

_____

 VS.

Winner: _____

_____

_____

For the glory of pizza!

EVENT LOG: NIGHT 4

Please report any unusual events in the space below.

INCIDENT REPORT

Date: _____ Time: _____ a.m./p.m.

Night Guard on Duty: _____

Person(s) Involved: _____

Animatronic(s) Involved: _____

Description of Events: _____

_____

Injury ☐ Property Damage ☐ Death ☐

Missing Persons ☐ Police Involved ☐

Signature _____

INCIDENT REPORT

Date: _____ Time: _____ a.m./p.m.

Night Guard on Duty: _____

Person(s) Involved: _____

Animatronic(s) Involved: _____

Description of Events: _____

_____

Injury ☐ Property Damage ☐ Death ☐

Missing Persons ☐ Police Involved ☐

Signature _____

INCIDENT REPORT

Date: _____ Time: _____ a.m./p.m.

Night Guard on Duty: _____

Person(s) Involved: _____

Animatronic(s) Involved: _____

Description of Events: _____

_____

Injury ☐ Property Damage ☐ Death ☐

Missing Persons ☐ Police Involved ☐

Signature _____

Feelings About Tonight's Shift

Please circle how you would rate your feelings on a scale of
1–10, with 10 being the best, and 1 being the worst, on the
scale below.

Overall: 1 2 3 4 5 6 7 8 9 10

Fulfillment: 1 2 3 4 5 6 7 8 9 10

I can hear sounds: 1 2 3 4 5 6 7 8 9 10

Stress: 1 2 3 4 5 6 7 8 9 10

Purpose: 1 2 3 4 5 6 7 8 9 10

Hope: 1 2 3 4 5 6 7 8 9 10

It was for me: 1 2 3 4 5 6 7 8 9 10

Welcome back to your last day on the job!
That is, the last day of your first week!
We can't believe you've made it this far—
what would it take to get you to come back next week?

_____

_____

_____

_____

_____

_____

_____

_____

_____

_____

_____

_____

_____

_____

_____

_____

_____

_____

You've earned your one-week bonus, which will be given to you in the form of a delightful gift basket, the cost of which will be taken out of your next paycheck. Design the gift basket you would like to receive in the space below.

This.

Not this.

If you had one piece of advice to give to the next night guard, what would it be?

_____
_____
_____
_____
_____
_____
_____
_____
_____
_____
_____
_____
_____
_____
_____
_____
_____

Would You Rather . . .

Dance with Ballora? . . . or . . . Sing with Circus Baby?

Spend all night in a
spring lock suit? . . . or . . . Spend all night in the dark?

Perform maintenance
on Funtime Freddy? . . . or . . . Try to fix Mangle?

Win a prize from the
Get a gift from the Puppet? . . . or . . . prize counter?

Try to outrun the Puppet? . . . or . . . Try to outrun Foxy?

Here at Freddy Fazbear's Pizza, many of our arcade machines use 8-bit graphics.
Use the grids below to convert Foxy into an 8-bit graphic!

Let's Eat!

Design an elaborate birthday cake for our patrons.
Detail the ingredients and steps to prepare it on the recipe
card on these pages. Then draw your design.

Ingredients

_____
_____
_____
_____
_____
_____
_____
_____
_____
_____
_____

Procedure

1. _____
   _____
   _____

2. _____
   _____
   _____

3. _____
   _____
   _____

4. _____
   _____
   _____

Draw your dish here.

Draw a birthday-themed animatronic worthy of delivering your new birthday cake in the space below.

When a PR disaster strikes, it's always good to have a plan. Think of alternate explanations to these common misunderstandings.

"My child said Freddy bit him!"

He tripped and fell on Freddy's teeth. Not our fault.

_____

_____

"That animatronic is filthy and oozing liquid!"

_____

_____

_____

"My child went missing in your pizzeria!"

_____

_____

_____

"My pizza has mold on it."

_____

_____

_____

Pretend you're an architect and imagine the optimal layout for a Freddy Fazbear's Pizza. Draw it here.

To celebrate the end of your first week, plan a party!
You can use the space below to get it organized.

Theme

Where

When

Decorations

Menu

People to Invite

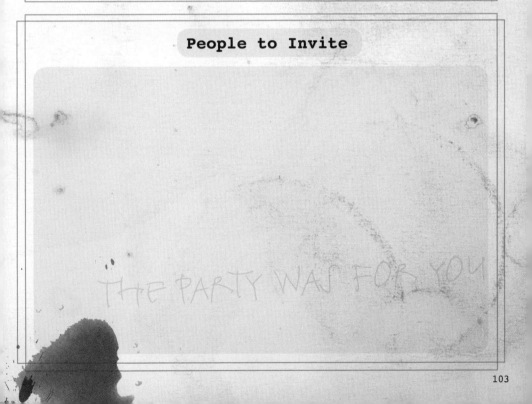

THE PARTY WAS FOR YOU

Create a newspaper article all about the life and accomplishments of a heroic security guard who perished in the line of duty, defending the pizzeria and its guests.

HEROIC SECURITY GUARD DEFENDS FUN FOR ALL

_____

_____

_____

_____

_____

_____

_____

_____

_____

_____

Draw or paste an image of yourself here.

_____

_____

_____

_____

_____

Draw all of your most valued treasures in the space below. Whom would you give each object to if you had to give them up?*

*Bonus: Consider seeking legal counsel to turn this list into a living will.

EVENT LOG: NIGHT 5

Please report any unusual events in the space below.

INCIDENT REPORT

Date: _____ Time: _____ a.m./p.m.

Night Guard on Duty: _____

Person(s) Involved: _____

Animatronic(s) Involved: _____

Description of Events: _____

_____

Injury ☐ Property Damage ☐ Death ☐

Missing Persons ☐ Police Involved ☐

Signature _____

INCIDENT REPORT

Date: _____ Time: _____ a.m./p.m.

Night Guard on Duty: _____

Person(s) Involved: _____

Animatronic(s) Involved: _____

Description of Events: _____

_____

Injury ☐ Property Damage ☐ Death ☐

Missing Persons ☐ Police Involved ☐

Signature _____

INCIDENT REPORT

Date: _____ Time: _8:11_ a.m./p.m.

Night Guard on Duty: _____

Person(s) Involved: _____

Animatronic(s) Involved: _____

Description of Events: _____

_____

Injury ☐ Property Damage ☐ Death ☐

Missing Persons ☐ Police Involved ☐

Signature _____

Feelings About Tonight's Shift

Please circle how you would rate your feelings on a scale of 1–10, with 10 being the best, and 1 being the worst, on the scale below.

Overall: 1 2 3 4 5 6 7 8 9 10

I can't see: 1 2 3 4 5 6 7 8 9 10

Health: 1 2 3 4 5 6 7 8 9 10

Stress: 1 2 3 4 5 6 7 8 9 10

I'm scared: 1 2 3 4 5 6 7 8 9 10

Hope: 1 2 3 4 5 6 7 8 9 10

Existential Dread: 1 2 3 4 5 6 7 8 9 10

SEE YOU
NEXT WEEK!

We at Fazbear Entertainment would like to thank you
for joining our company. We hope this logbook helped you
get a better handle on your responsibilities and also provided
a bit of fun for you at the end of a long shift.

It's no small feat to survive the daily grind here, and we
commend you for your courage and lack of common sense.
Until next time!